For my Mother and Best Friend, Justine Wise

And I would like to thank Jean K. for her great ideas and encouragement to keep going.

-Norma

For Glen and Carrie
- Brenda

Thunder Hill
P u b l i s h i n g

Proudly published by Thunder Hill Publishing. Copyright 2010.

All rights reserved. No part of this book may be copied, reproduced, or used without permission of artist and author.

For more information, contact the publisher at www.EricEbinger.com

Foreword

    Within moments of meeting Norma Wise, I felt like we had been friends for a very long time. Stories have a way of bringing people together quickly. At least stories shared with the warmth, affection, and hilarious tone of what we now call Wise Cracks. Between the laughter, Norma leaned over and said to me with her hand on my arm, "I want to tell these stories and make people laugh."
    Good things happen to good people like Norma. And a few months into our partnership, she was introduced to a woman with a knack for drawing. Norma shared her stories, and Brenda Morse said she immediately saw the pictures in her head. When the first drawing came over the fax machine, Norma said, "I knew it was a match."
    The three of us have shared meals where one story leads to another, which leads to another, and another. And we hope this book serves as the same tickler for you and your family. Included within are blank pages intended for you to record your own stories. What a lasting treasure for your family!
    It has been a privilege to work with Norma and Brenda, and bring these stories and drawings to pages which can be shared and passed and laughed over in the living room. There is great joy in the telling and in the drawing; we hope there is joy in reading, too.

Eric Ebinger

All the stories you are about to read are true.

They are stories from family, friends, and some even from total strangers. I just overheard them talking at restaurants, ballgames, or just shopping.

The names have all been changed to protect the innocent.

After meeting Brenda and receiving her first drawing, I knew it was a match; my stories just came to life. I laughed from the first picture and we have not stopped laughing.

Hopefully this is the start of many more "Wise Cracks."

-Norma

Here Kitty, Kitty

Sandy and Julie were doing dishes. The window is directly over the sink. In the backyard, they could hear the kids playing. All of a sudden, they hear one of the kids say, "Make your eyes big, Kitty!" Both Mothers run outside and see Julie's four year old daughter holding the cat tight around his middle, his eyes pleading for help.

Cat free… daughter in a time out… life is good again.

(No animals were hurt in this story)

Thanks for the Diet Dinner

Sue was invited to a friends for a pork chop dinner. It was one of the girls' birthday and they were all getting together to celebrate. Sue told them she would not be eating, but have cake and ice cream only. Well, they bought Sue a dinner and got it ready for Sue when she was leaving, placing a piece of cake on top.

When she got home and opened the container, there was some old pork chop bones, leftover potatoes and a half eaten roll. They put the garbage in the bag instead of the dinner. When everyone was gone, they realized they had an extra dinner. Way too much fun laughing about the dinner. Sue would never hurt anyone's feelings; when asked she said it was delicious.

Lost a little weight on that meal.

To Eat or Not to Eat

Steve went to visit his ninety five year old great aunt who had just been diagnosed with diabetes. When Steve got there, she was eating a large piece of chocolate cake. He said, "Aunt Grace, you should not be eating that cake." She looked at him and said, "Sonny, I'm going to die from eating it at my age, not die from wanting it."

You go, girl.

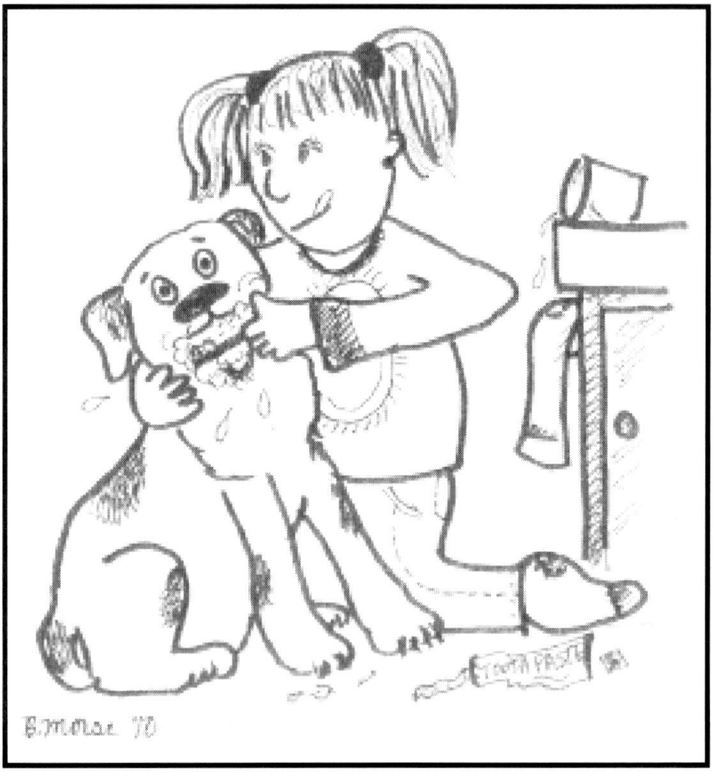
TOOTH PASTE
B.McMae '10

Use Mine

Ned caught his daughter in the bathroom using HIS toothbrush to brush the dog's teeth. He asked her about it and she said, "Dad I do it all the time!"

His toothbrush is now put up Very High.

Help Me, Please

Randy got a new vest for Christmas. One day after the holiday he was going shopping. Before he got out of the car, he put on his hat and scarf, but forgot his gloves. He was walking toward the store and put his hands in his vest.

When he got to the door, he realized he could not get his hands out of the vest pockets. Every time he would pull on his hands, the vest would go up. He finally went inside and asked someone to help hold the vest so he could pull out his hands.

How embarrassing!

Record your memories here!

Record your memories here!

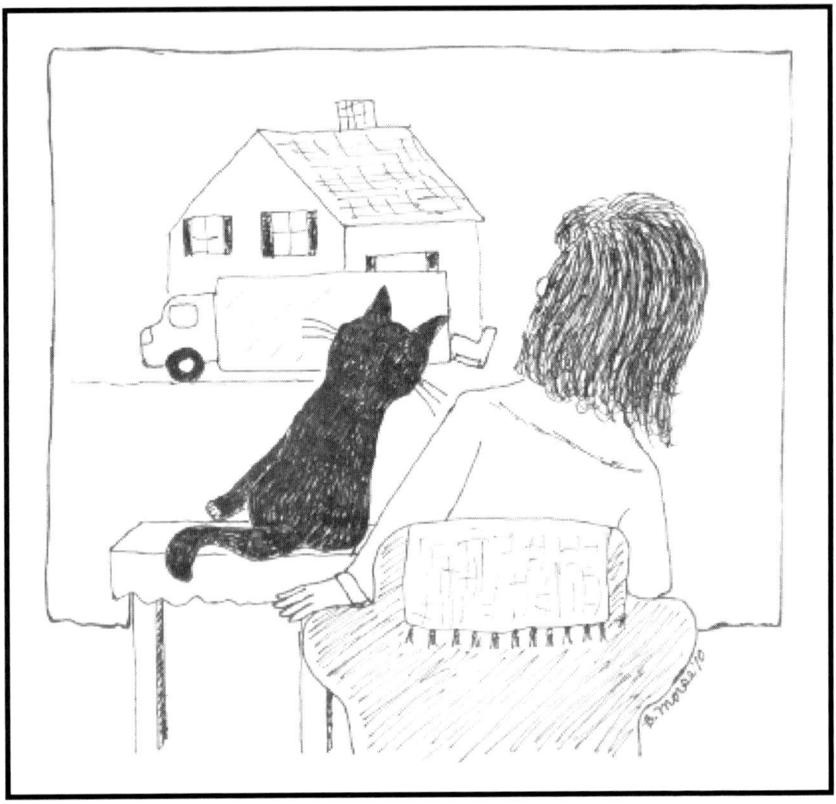

We are not nosey…

June was sitting in her chair looking out the front window watching the neighbors move in across the street. She weaved back and forth to get the best look. Beside her on a table was her cat, also watching the neighbors move in, also weaving back and forth.

The two of them are definitely spending too much time together.

Whose Gift is This?

Tom changed ALL the name tags on the Christmas presents the night before Christmas after everyone was in bed. This was really funny to everyone but his Mom, who spent hours wrapping and putting the name tags on each present.

What a Christmas, everyone was opening everyone else's gifts!

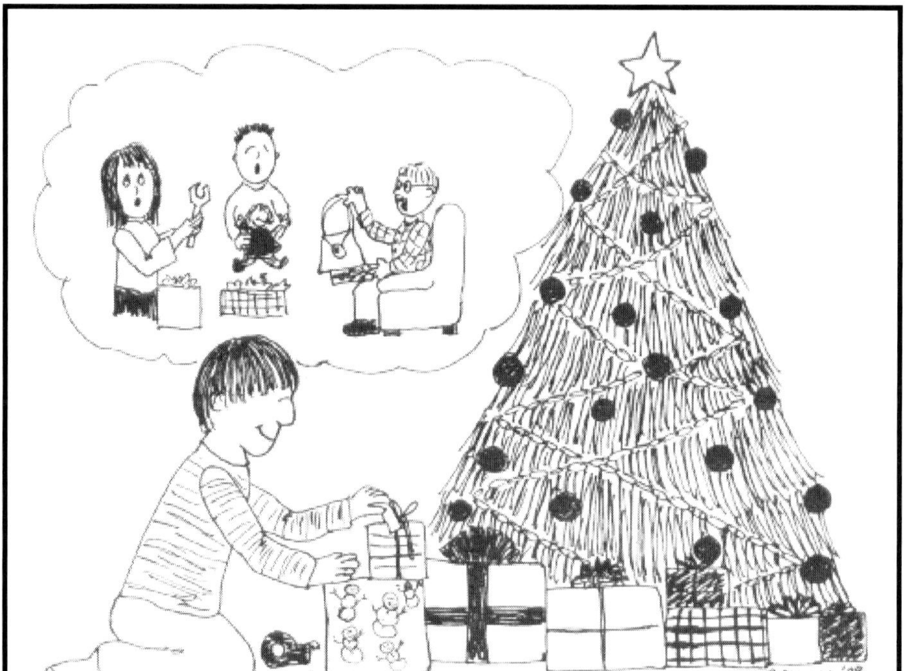

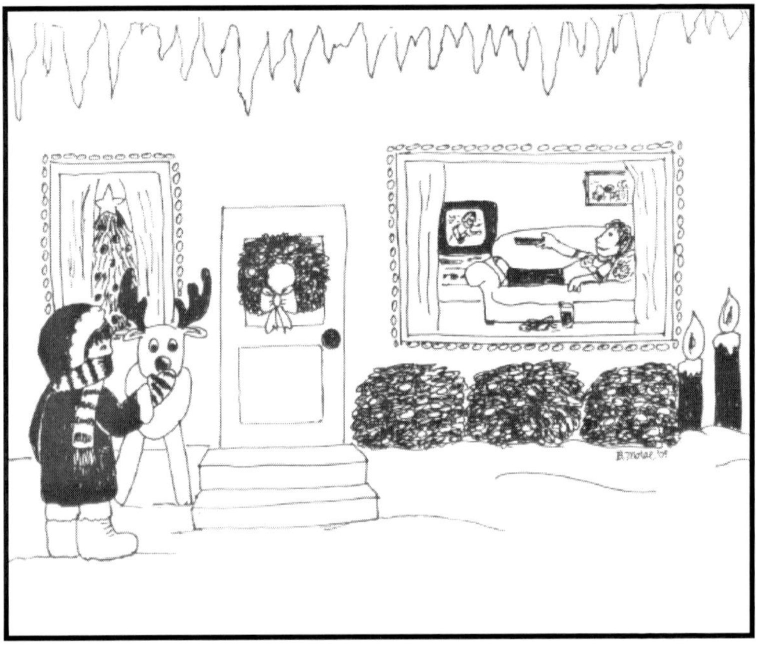

Christmas Decorations

Beth was putting up Christmas decorations on one of the coldest weekends we ever had. She would put up a few, then go inside and get warm. Her husband was inside laying on the couch watching football. The decorations looked great. The following weekend was the judging of the decorations. In the newspaper, her husband's name was listed under the Honorable Mention.

I'm sure he helped take them down.

I'm Sorry…

Sara went to the movies. The movie had already started, so Sara quickly took her seat. When she sat down, she missed the cup holder and her drink ran all the way down the rows.

Unfortunately, her boss and his wife were three rows down, with her drink running right down the floor towards them. When the movie was finished, Sara quickly ran out before she got caught.

Free Me, Please

Judy's dog is so dumb. He broke loose from his chain the other day and just stayed in the yard. He didn't realize he could finally take off.

Maybe next time, Bud.

You ARE Gonna Share

At Sue's office every year at Christmastime, salesman bring in large trays of meats and cheese's. Unfortunately, three girls in the office are way in the back office and never got any treats. One day, they saw the salesman arrive. They sent Sue to the main office to load up her pockets. She had so much meat and cheese they could hardly eat it all! But next time, she might want to put it in something besides her pockets, she smelled of salami and swiss cheese the rest of the day.

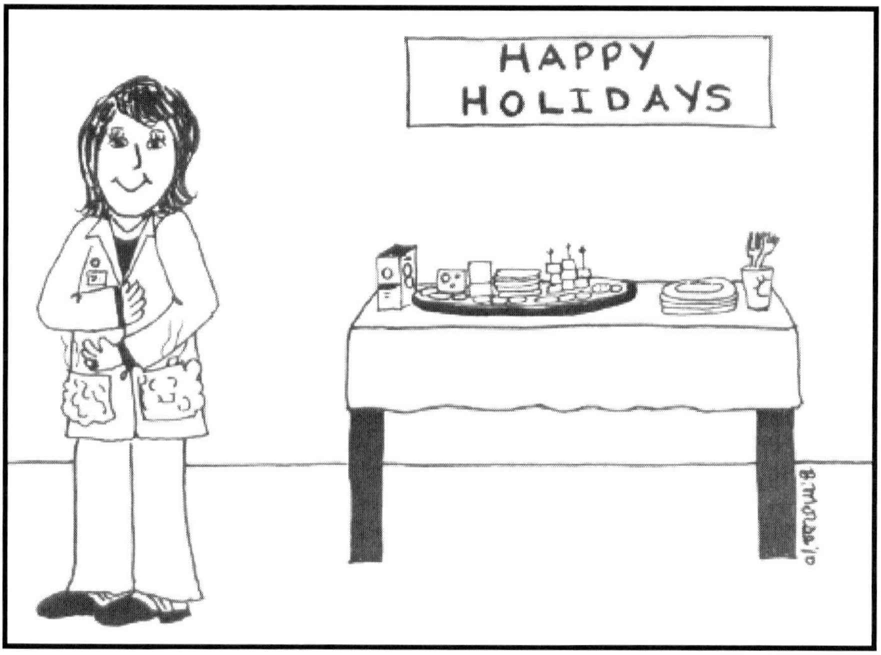
HAPPY HOLIDAYS

Love My New Coat

Taylor was walking around the mall with her husband in her new BLACK wool coat she had bought three weeks earlier. She really liked the looks of the coat, and it felt great, too. She was walking through one of the stores when she noticed on an overhead mirror something on the back of her coat. OH NO… there it was. Baby Puke from one of her grandchildren the week before.

Yes. White and streaming halfway down the new BLACK wool coat. Oh well, that's the way it goes. It really did look good for a while.

She really wants to thank her husband for pointing it out to her.

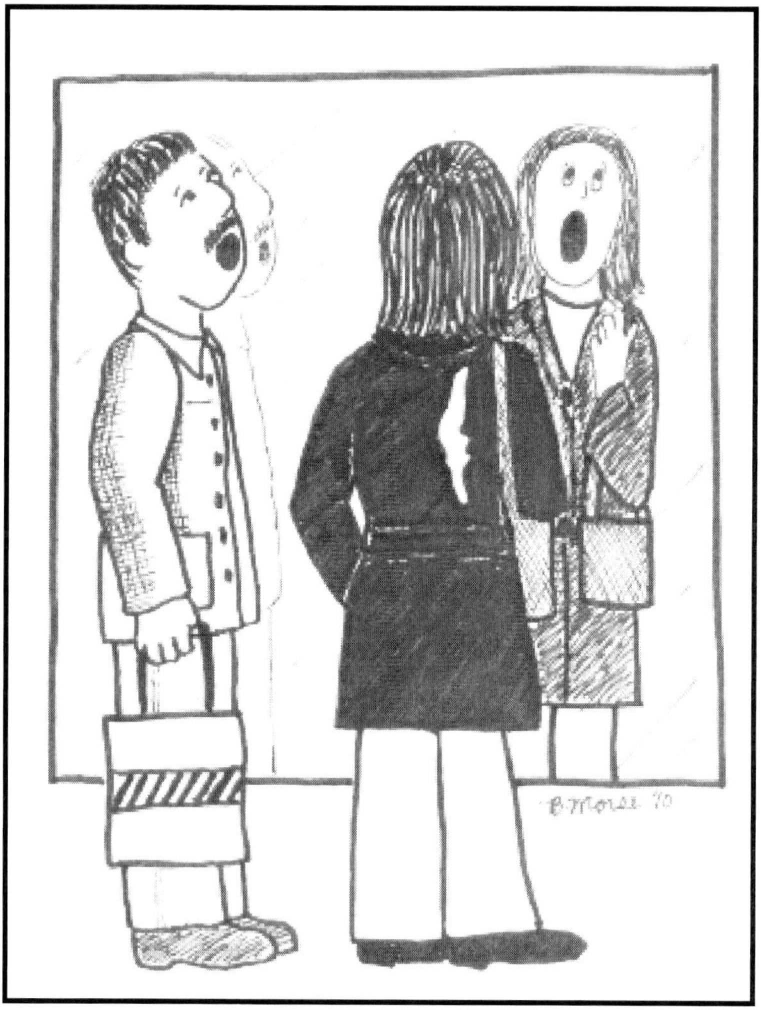
B Morse '70

My Life Passed Before Me

We were sitting at a softball game when my daughter, who had about four pieces of bright blue bubble gum in her mouth, tried to blow a bubble. The gum blew out of her mouth into the hair of the blond lady sitting in front of her. Everyone saw it and started to laugh, but the lady never felt it.

What to do?

I tapped the lady on the shoulder and said, "Ma'am, a leaf just blew in your hair. I will get it out for you."

I gently took it out, and life was good again.

Twins

Mary had twin daughters, age eight. At school, they were having a rummage sale. The girls were given $1 to spend on anything they wanted. They both wanted clothes. Later that day, I saw them in a store. One girl had on a matching skirt, blouse and vest. I asked her Mom, "Where is her sister?" Her Mom replied, "You will know her when you see her."

Just then, she came around the corner wearing a beautiful formal, about five sizes too big for her. But she thought it was beautiful.

You just have to love us women.

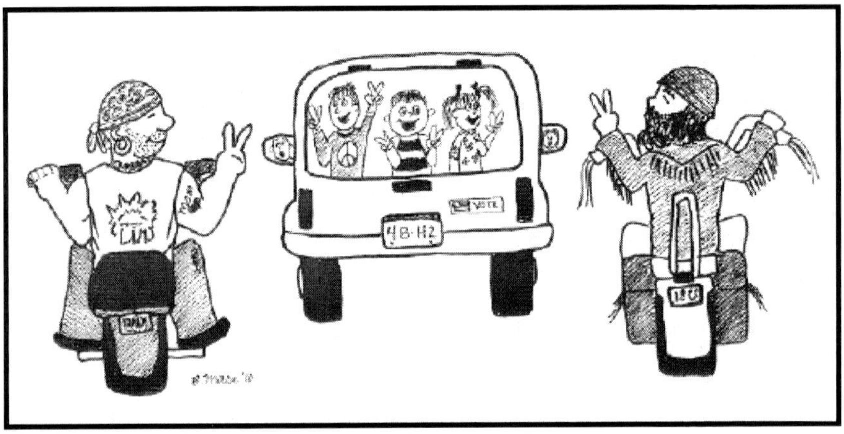
VOTE
4B·142

Peace Out, Man

Years ago, Randy and Beth were riding down a four lane highway in their old blue station wagon. The back seat was facing traffic. All of a sudden, Randy noticed his three little kids giving the peace sign to a motorcycle gang right behind them. The group of motorcyclists pulled up beside them and with a big smile, gave Randy and Beth the peace sign.

Flying Wallendas

Pat had seven children and lived in a two story home. On each step going upstairs, Pat put the kid's names. Then she would place their laundry, mail and anything else for them to pick up as they went upstairs.

One day when she was passing in front of the steps, she saw one of the girls jumping about five steps so she wouldn't have o take anything else that didn't belong to her. Heaven forbid she take anyone else's things with her!

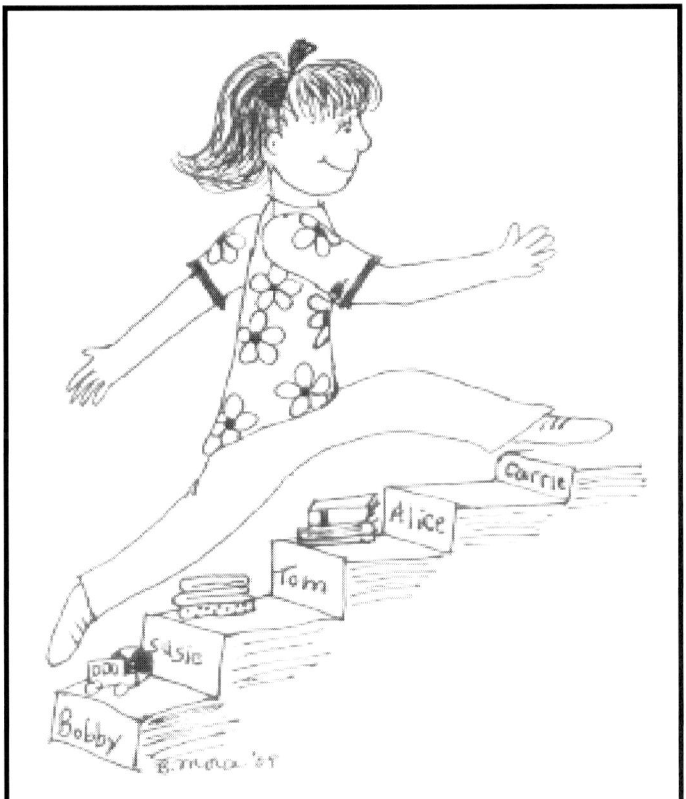
Carrie
Alice
Tom
Susie
Bobby

Record your memories here!

Record your memories here!

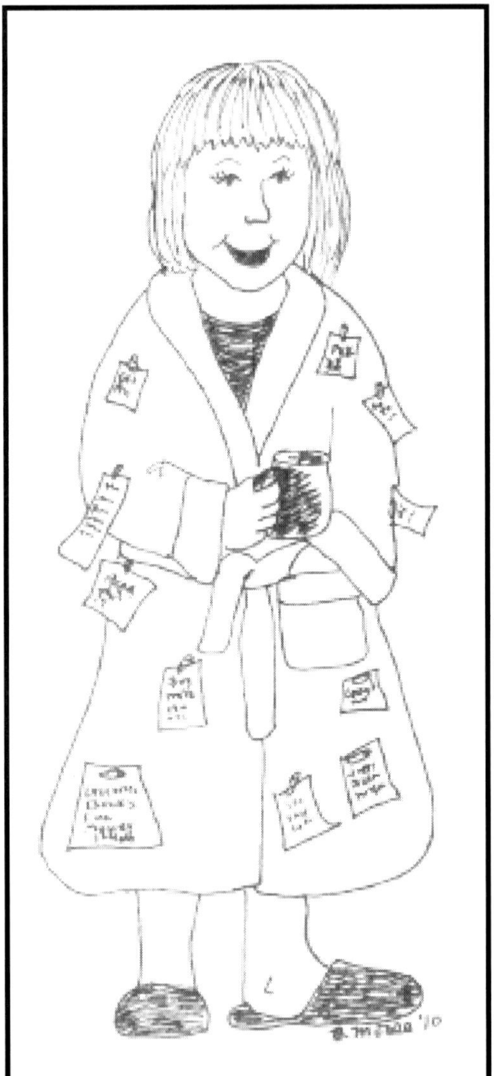

Go Read Mom…

Nancy said growing up was such a hassle. Everyone is busy with school projects, sports, etc. She said at night before they would go to bed, they would go and read Mom.

You see, her Mom had her own way of remembering things. (This was before Post It Notes.) She would jot things down on a piece of paper for each child; then pin it to her long bathrobe… (that she was wearing at the time!)

Halloween

One Halloween we put a dummy on the front porch. Every night, the neighborhood kids would throw it over the porch. John finally decided to come up with a plan. So he dressed up in the dummy's clothes. When he heard footsteps, he knew, "Here they come!"

When the neighborhood kids stepped on the porch, he jumped! And they are probably still running.

They were so scared. Revenge is so sweet.

Wish Me a Happy Birthday Bus Driver

Beth was a bus driver. One of the kids getting on the bus said to her, "Would you like one of my birthday treats?" Beth held out her hand waiting for some candy. But instead, he dropped a small cup full of Lime Jell-O. She hates Lime Jell-O! But she did not want to hurt his feelings; so she plopped the whole thing in her mouth.

Yuk… Yes, Lime Jell-O does leave an aftertaste. CANDY next time, please.

I'll Be There Shortly!!

Brenda was eighty years old, her mom was in a nursing home at age 101. Her body was failing, but her mind was great. Brenda's Dad passed away when she was ten years old. Every year on the fourth of July, they would both put flowers on her grave.

The year she turned 101, they went out to the cemetery and Brenda's Mom put her head on Brenda's shoulder and said "I bet Daddy thinks I'm not coming."

What a sense of humor even at 101.

Sweeper Don't Give Up

Beth's kids were out in the woods behind their house and came upon a large hive of some kind. They wanted to keep it and Beth said, "Ok, but leave it outside tonight."

One of the boys went out and got it and brought it in the house. In the morning, Beth woke up to probably one million Praying Mantis bugs all over the house.

Everyone was in charge of cleaning them up. They were EVERYWHERE!

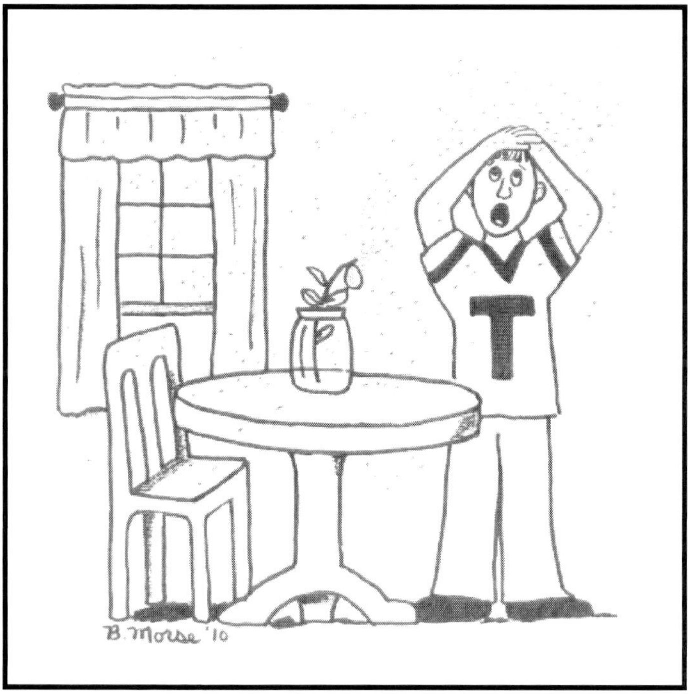
B. Morse '10

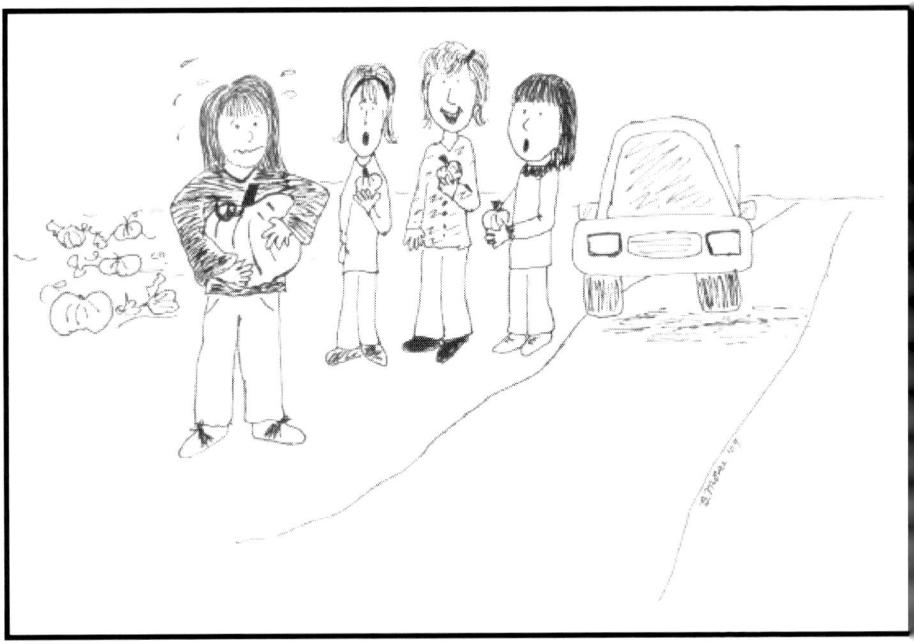

Stealing Pumpkins

Several girls were out one night when they decided to steal pumpkins. One girl drove the car while the rest went into the pumpkin patch. (Did I mention it was one of the girl's grandparents fields.) What a challenge. They ran the huge patch and then everyone met back at the car.

Nancy was out of breath when she realized she had stolen the biggest pumpkin in the patch! The rest of them had pumpkins the size of apples.

The things we go through to save a Buck.

Thanksgiving Headband

Angela was in a Thanksgiving play at school. All the Indians wore colorful headbands. That night, she rolled her chewing gum in a long rope and wrapped it around her little brother's forehead.

Now, ALL mouths are checked before bedtime.

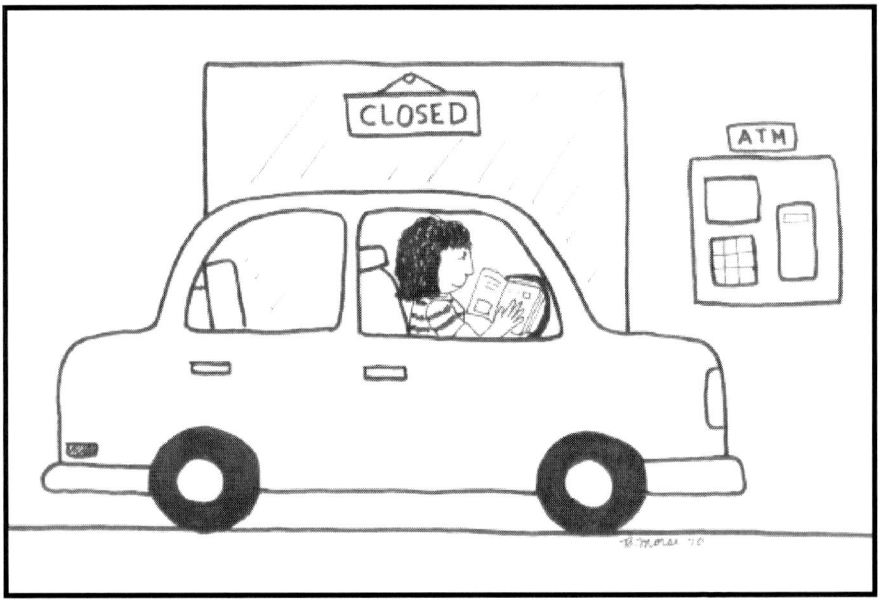
CLOSED
ATM

Columbus Day

Janet was going to the bank as she usually did on Monday. She grabbed her paperback book and headed out. She got to the drive in bank and sat there… waiting for the girl to send out the container.

She sat there and sat there, reading quite a while. All of a sudden, she looked into the bank and noticed there were no lights on inside. Yes, most banks are closed on Columbus Day.

Unfortunately, she came back to work and told everyone. She at least had a nice long break.

(Maybe she knew it was closed?)

Unforgettable

Sally was about four years old when she got a new tricycle. She was riding around and around the house. The family was going to supper so they all packed into the car. They got to the end of the street and realized they forgot Sally. When they returned to the house, there she was; riding around and around the house.

They promised they would never forget her again, but needless to say her brothers and sisters never let her forget it!

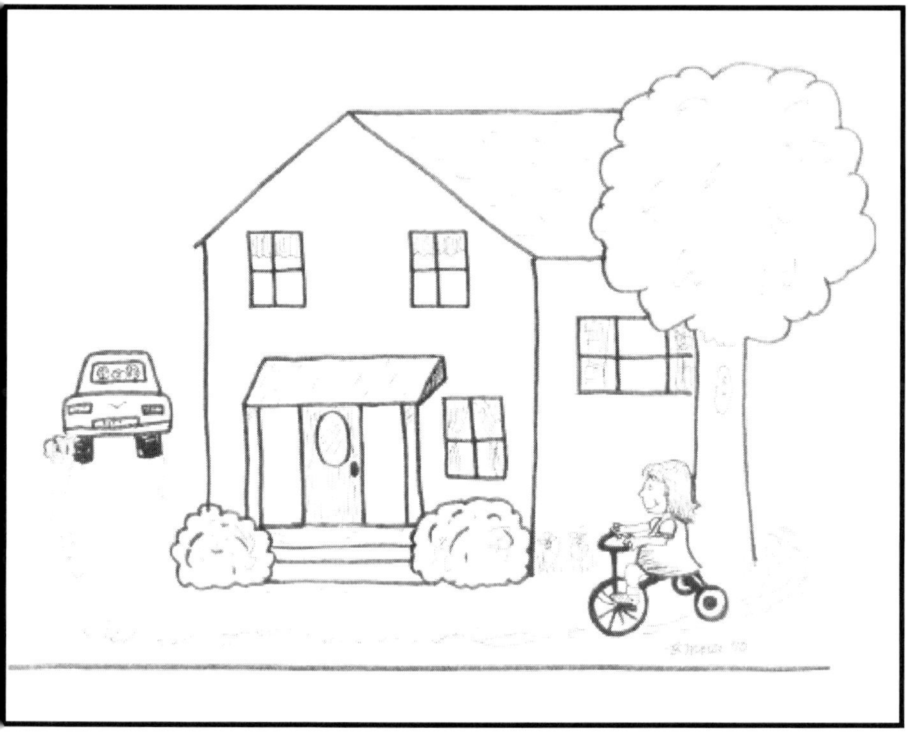

Record your memories here!

Record your memories here!

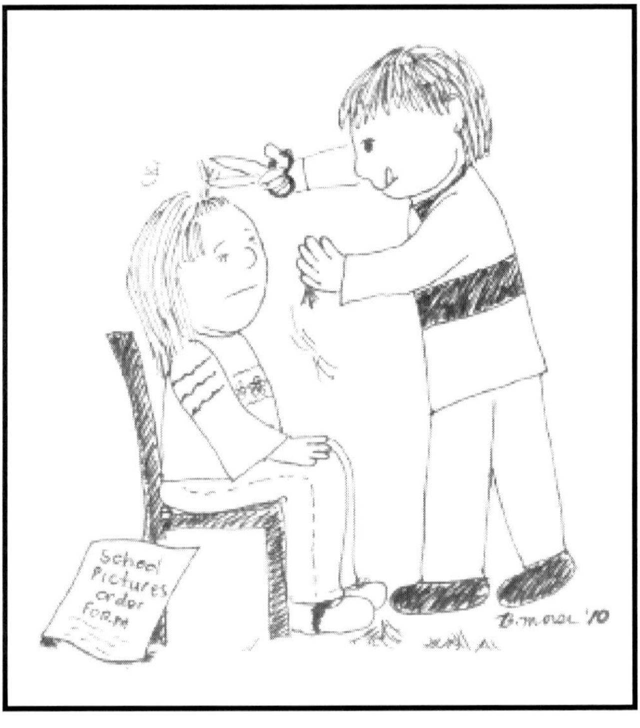
School Pictures order Form
B.m.aa '10

School Pictures

Beth put the kids to bed, ages six and seven. She always checked their mouths for gum. One horrible night, Tess lied and hid her gum. Somehow, during the night, the gum went from her mouth to her hair.

In the morning, her brother helped her out so she wouldn't get in trouble. He cut her bangs. Afterwards, there was nothing they could do. Her bangs were a quarter of an inch long.

Beautiful.

Happy Birthday

Nancy was in a restaurant when she saw a little boy sitting down from her. He was about five years old, and in front of him were five tubs of sour cream and a soda. The rest of the family was at the buffet.

Throughout dinner, Nancy kept staring at the boy to the point that the mother looked at her and said, "I am so embarrassed. It is his birthday and he can go anywhere and eat anything he wants. He wanted to go to his favorite restaurant and get sour cream and a soda."

She told Nancy when they get home they are going to have cake and ice cream.

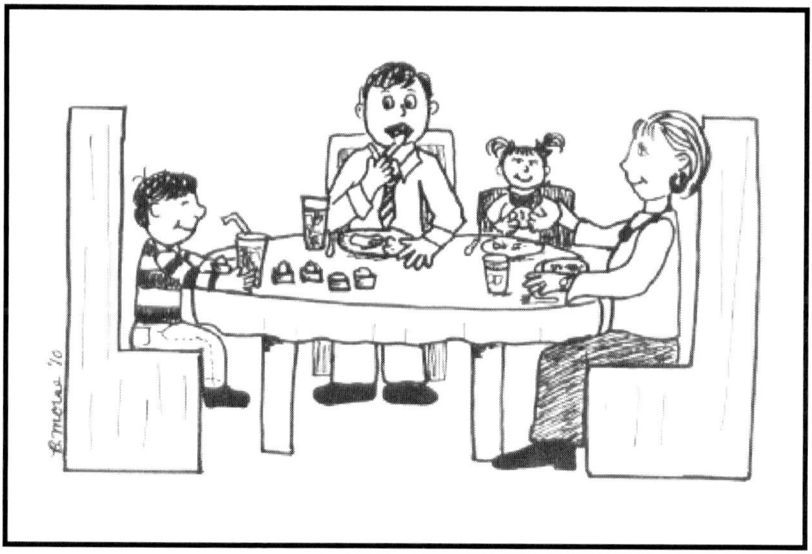

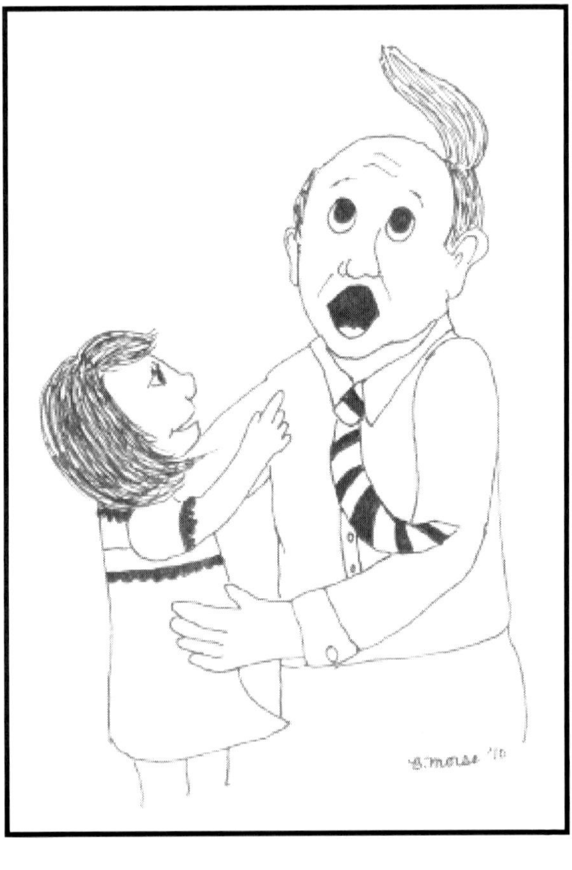

Wind Wind Go Away

Randy was one of those men who parted his hair just over his ear and combed it over the top of his head, then sprayed it so it wouldn't move. On a windy day, his granddaughter came over to visit.

They were sitting outside at the picnic table, when a blast of wind blew over them. Randy's hair went straight up in the air! His granddaughter looked at him and said, "Grandpa, your hair is broken!"

Uh-Oh, is this your gift?

Last Christmas, Peggy got sick of the kids trying to look at their name tags and peek at their packages to see what they were going to get. So, she came up with an idea to make a list of the gifts and put numbers on it, so there were no names... just numbers.

Sounds like the ideal system, doesn't it?

And it would have been if Peggy did not lose the list.

But fortunately, her family reminds her EVERY Christmas.

Short Story

On Monday, John was to write a report on what he did on Sunday. John wrote,

"Rain- No Game- The End."

We Won!! We Won!!

Tom and his friend were always driving everyone crazy with their jokes. A couple days before the county fair, the boys stole two flowers from the neighbor's flower garden. They entered them in the fair. One of the boys won second place, the other honorable mention.

Who says it doesn't pay to steal? Boys, boys boys!!

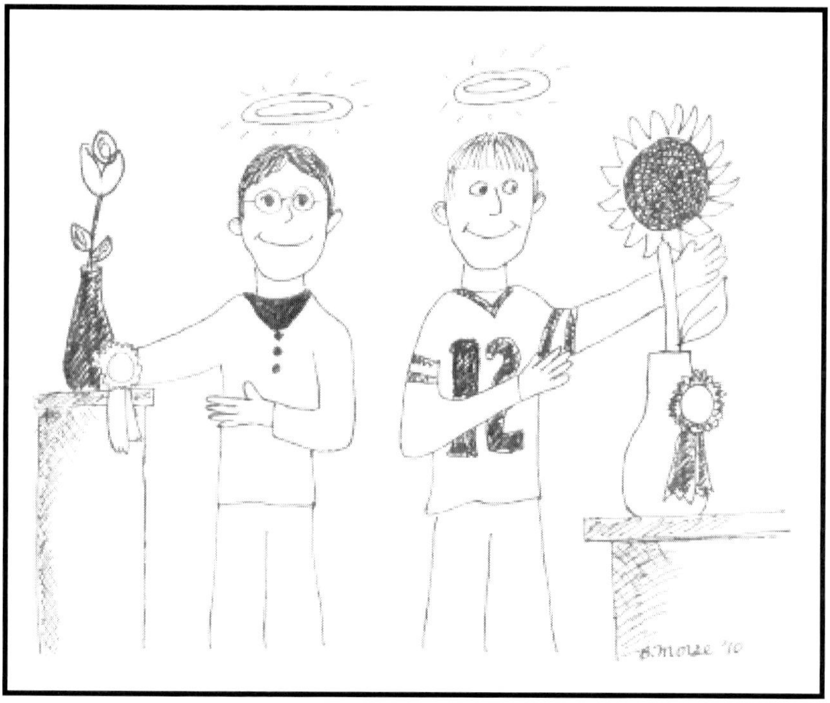
12
B.Motze '10

Flower Pot or Hammock

Judy ordered a macramé hanging flower pot. When it arrived in the mail, it turned out to be a macramé hammock. (The girl has no trees). So she brought it to work to see if anyone wanted to buy it. She worked in an office with ten girls, two of them worked in the back office where no one usually saw them.

The back office girls grabbed the hammock, put it on the bracket of a door jam, then grabbed Judy and put her in the hammock. All of a sudden, they heard footsteps. The two girls ran, but Judy was stuck. She stayed there while the boss walked by her and said, "Hi Judy!" and kept going.

The guilty parties know who they are.

I Love My Sister

Chrissy, age thirteen, was upstairs. Her sister Julie, age fifteen was downstairs. All of a sudden, Julie's phone rang. It was her sister, upstairs. She wanted her to bring her a drink. Of course, being the wonderful sister she is, she quickly ran to the refrigerator, grabbed a cold soda and ran it upstairs to her sister.

You don't believe this do you?

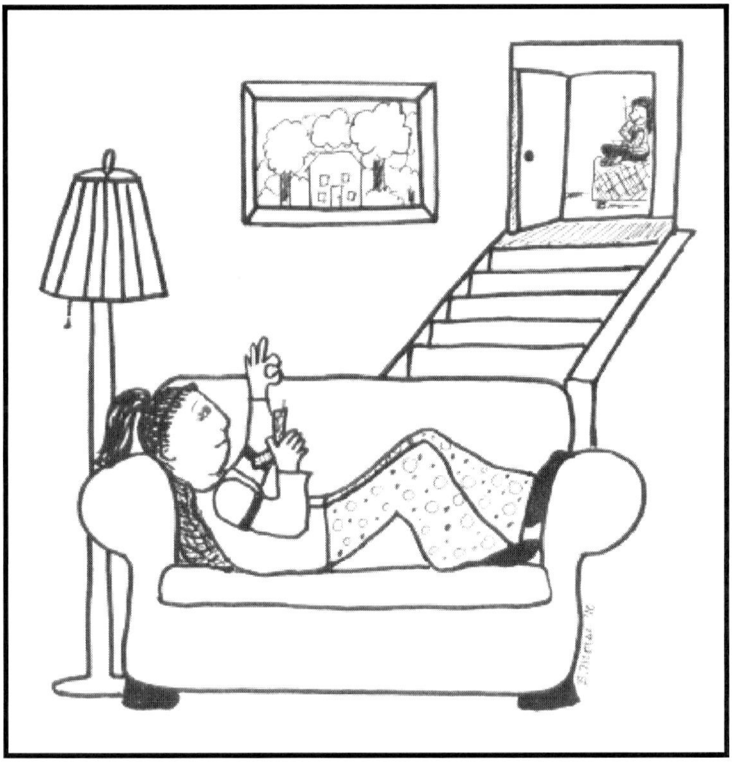

Do Not Help Her With Homework

Jan (age ten) was working on her homework. Tom came home and said, "Let me help you." She said she was working on their nationality. She then asked him where the family came from. He said, "Your Grandma was from Ohio and your other Grandma was from West Virginia, so I guess you are a Hillbillian."

Jan wrote that down.

The next day, the teacher read Jan's paper. The teacher went to school with Jan's Dad. She told Jan, "Please DO NOT let your Dad help with your homework again."

So Tom is banned from helping.

What an Impression

Randy finally got the new car all by himself. He was sixteen and proud as he could be. He rode around uptown, everyone he knew was there!

Right in front of the courthouse downtown, the light changed to red. He jumped out of the car, ran around the car and then jumped back in again, with everyone watching him!

Unfortunately, this car was a FOUR door, not a TWO door, and he jumped in the backseat all by himself. He then had to get out of the car and get in the front seat. Yes, everyone was laughing. Hard to live these things down.

He laughs about it now. (I think.)

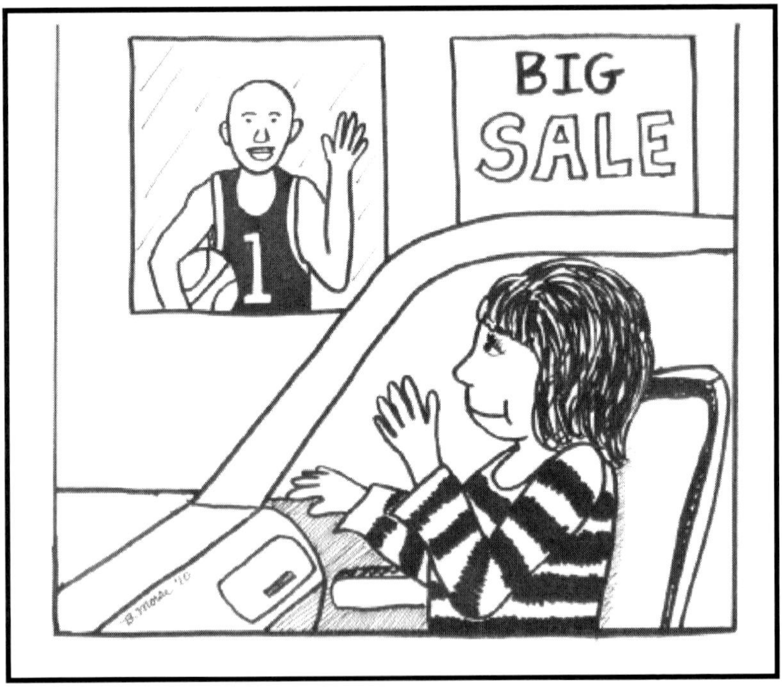
1
BIG
SALE
B. Moser '10

Who's Waving to Me?

Nancy and her Mom, Joyce, were riding around downtown when Joyce waved to someone in a store. Nancy asked, "Who was that?" and Joyce answered, "I'm not sure. We have many relatives."

Nancy turned around and went back. And there it was, a giant poster of Shaquille O'Neal holding up a sign of a sale going on in the store.

Shaquille, you are in luck. You are not a relative of ours.

Everyone Wake Up

Sharon lived several hours from her parents. She would come home every weekend to help them out, but they would always be asleep. She decided to get them a dog. She bought a small wild terrier, bowls, leash, etc. She thought it would be great for them to walk him. For several weeks they were walking the dog. The fifth week, she came home. Mom asleep in her recliner; Dad asleep on the couch and the dog asleep in his bed.

So much for that idea.

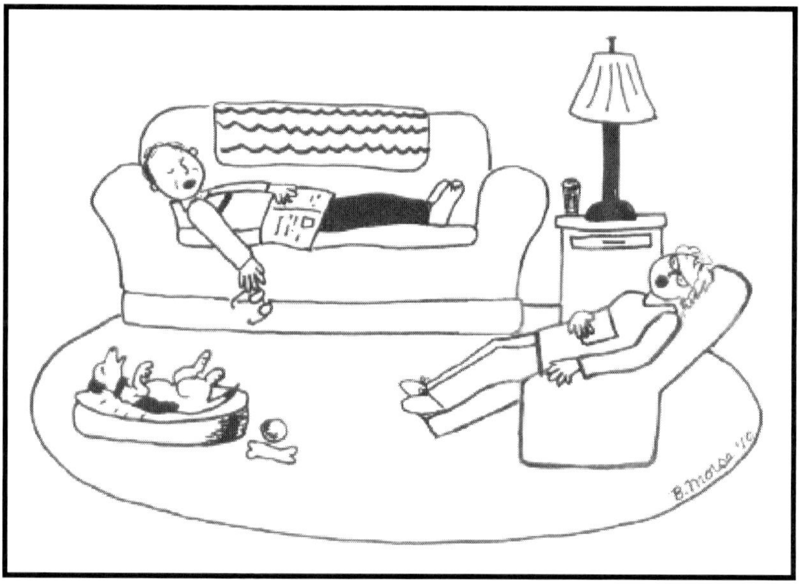

Record your memories here!

Record your memories here!

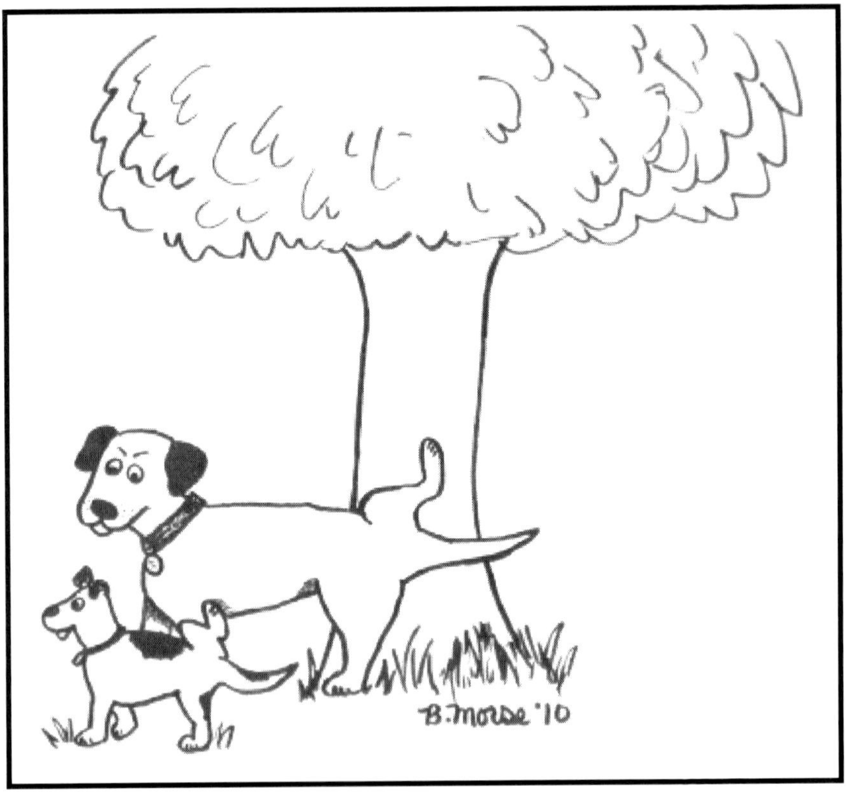
B.Morse '10

Go Outside and Do Your Business

Peppy and Spanky, the family male dogs, were sent outside to do their business. Beth looked out and there was Peppy, lifting his leg on the big tree outside. And there, was Spanky, lifting his leg on Peppy. Poor boys, they both had to come in and get a bath.

Remember, boys, watch where you're going.

The Stars Called

Mom was driving with Grandma. Mom's car had a stick-shift. Unfortunately, it was an icy day and they were trying to get up a hill. Then, the car started to stall and was going backwards.

Mom yelled, "THE STARS CALLED! THE STARS CALLED!"

Grandma said, "What did they say?"

Of course, she meant to say, "The car stalled." No more stick shifts at this house.

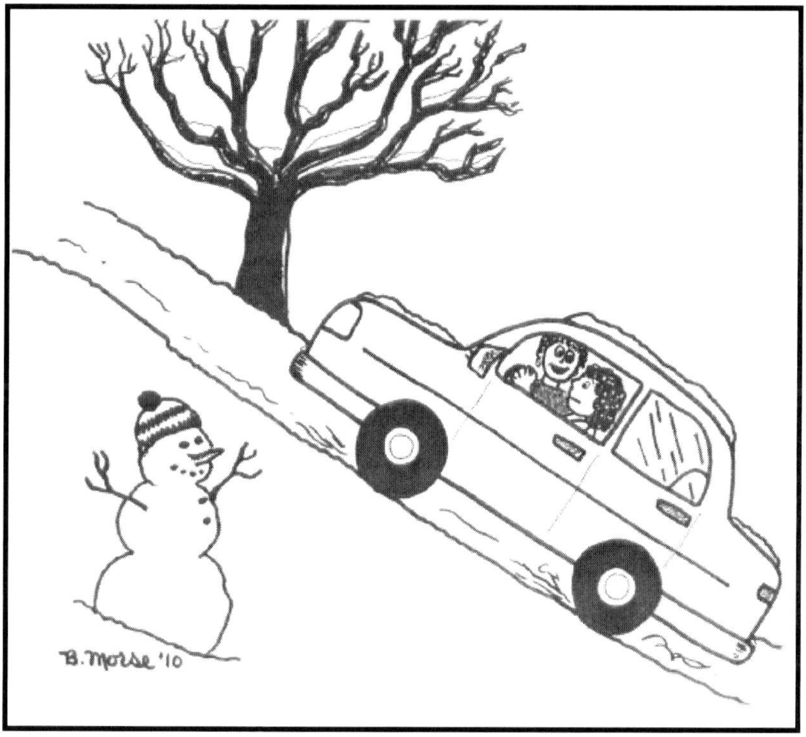
B. Morse '10

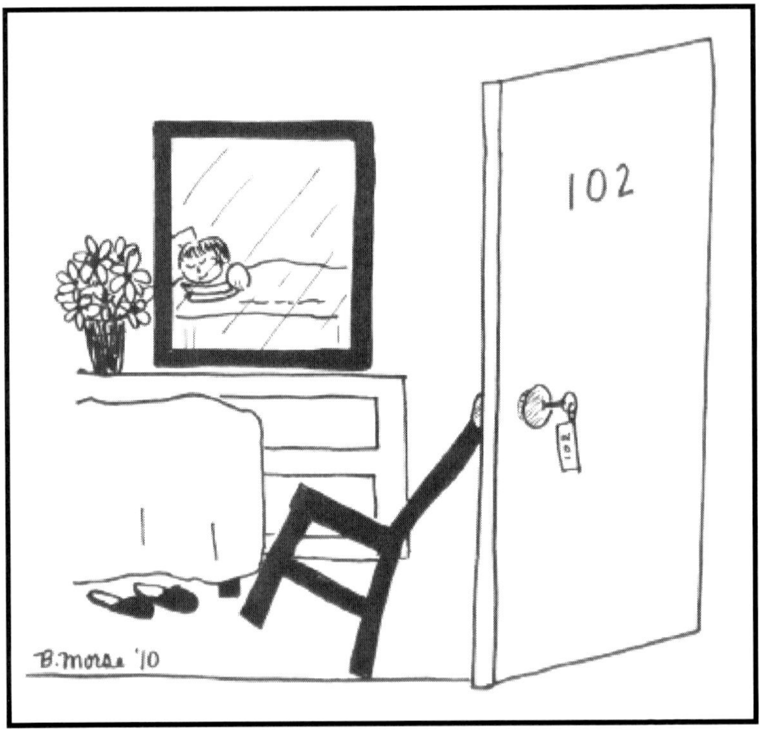
102
B.Morse '10

World Wide Travelers

Nancy and her Mom were going to Amish country for the weekend. They had gotten the room and were tired and ready to spend the night. Nancy took a chair and put it under the door knob so no one could get inside the room while they slept.

The next morning, they removed the chair and opened the door. There, in the OUTSIDE door knob was the key.

What are you doing?

On our major trash pick up, two women were riding around in a pick up, looking for good stuff. One of the women was about to become a Grandma for the first time. They saw this small chest of drawers, just what they needed.

They backed the truck up and started to load it when a woman came SCREAMING out of the house, "What are you DOING?"

It seems the lady was just moving and it was NOT for the trash pick up.

Oops. They made an embarrassed get away.

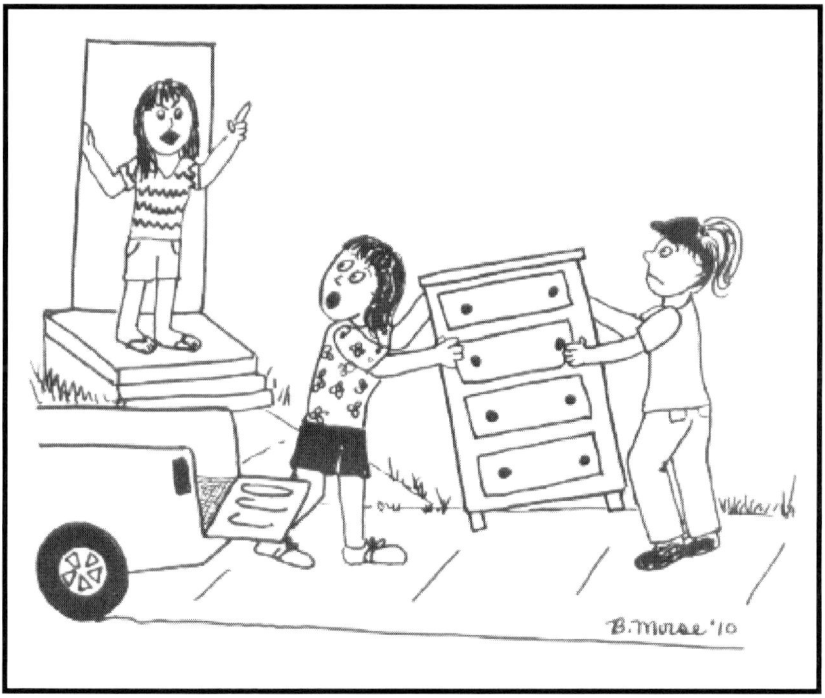

Record your memories here!

Record your memories here!

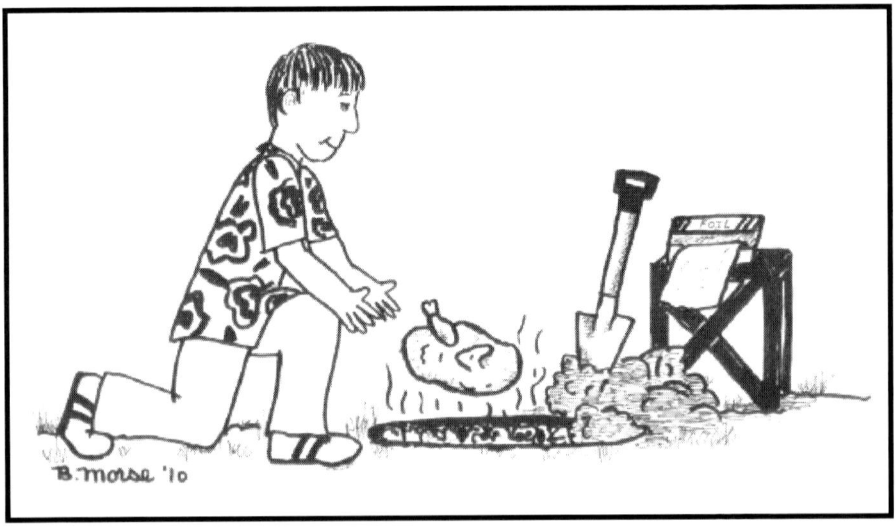
FOIL
B. Morse '10

Yum Yum

Rick got a new magazine in the mail and read the article on cooking. He learned how to dig a hole and cook a chicken in it. So Rick followed the directions and then took the family to the park.

Everyone was excited at what awaited them when they got home, especially Mom. They pulled in the driveway, ran to the backyard, dug up the dirt anticipating the results… and to their surprise found a completely raw chicken and cold coals. Who knew?

Disappointment- Yes.

Pizza for Supper- Yes.

You Look Guilty

Rick's family owned a white VW bus. Rick was an honor student, into sports, and a clean cut kid. He was on an errand for his Dad, driving the bus out of town.

The police stopped him and took him out of the vehicle. Unfortunately, there was a robbery in town and the driver had the same vehicle Rick was driving!

At least, that is the story he told us.

Acknowledgements

To Lisa Wise:
Thanks for bringing Brenda, Eric and I together.

To Tim, Justina and Cass:
Thanks for reading my stories and making me laugh when you read them.

To Brenda:
Your pictures have brought my stories to life. I knew from the first picture we were going to be friends and partners.

To Eric:
You have always been there for all my questions and calls. Please don't move or change your phone number.

To everyone in the book, you know who you are; you have all made me laugh through the years.
                                        -Norma

Thank you to my family and friends who have always supported my creative endeavors. A special thank you to everyone who asks me to help with your projects by drawing, gluing, cutting, sewing, coloring, etc.!
                                        -Brenda